ARACHNID WORLD
MITES

SANDRA MARKLE

MASTER SNEAKS

LERNER PUBLICATIONS COMPANY MINNEAPOLIS

FOR CURIOUS KIDS EVERYWHERE

ACKNOWLEDGMENTS

The author would like to thank Dr. Barry O'Connor, University of Michigan; Dr. Elena Rhodes, University of Florida; and Dr. Simon Pollard, Canterbury Museum, Christchurch, New Zealand, for sharing their expertise and enthusiasm. A special thanks to Skip Jeffery for his support during the creation of this book.

Lerner Publications Company
A division of Lerner Publishing Group, Inc.
241 First Avenue North
Minneapolis, MN 55401 U.S.A.

Website address: www.lernerbooks.com

Library of Congress Cataloging-in-Publication Data

Markle, Sandra.
    Mites : master sneaks / by Sandra Markle.
        p.   cm. — (Arachnid world)
    Includes bibliographical references and index.
    ISBN 978–0–7613–5046–0 (lib. bdg. : alk. paper)
    1. Mites—Juvenile literature. I. Title.
  QL458.M366 2012
  595.4'2—dc23   2011021462

Manufactured in the United States of America
1 - DP - 12/31/11

CONTENTS

AN ARACHNID'S WORLD

WELCOME TO THE WORLD OF ARACHNIDS

(ah-RACK-nidz). Arachnids can be found in every habitat on Earth except in the deep ocean. Some are even found in Antarctica.

So how can you tell if an animal is an arachnid rather than a relative like an insect? Both belong to a group of animals called arthropods (AR-throh-podz). The animals in this group share some traits. They have bodies divided into segments, jointed legs, and a stiff exoskeleton. This is a skeleton on the outside like a suit of armor. But one way to tell if an animal is an arachnid is to count its legs and body parts. While not every adult arachnid has eight legs, most do. Arachnids also usually have two main body parts. Most adult insects, like this louse *(right)*, have six legs and three main body parts.

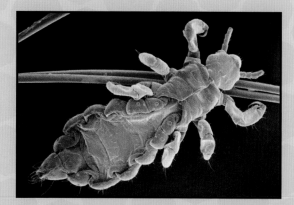

This book is about arachnids called mites. A few kinds are as big as raisins. But most, like these dust mites *(facing page)*, are tiny—smaller than the period at the end of this sentence. Some are plant eaters. Some are predators (hunters). And some are parasites, living off other living things. But all mites thrive by taking advantage of their small size.

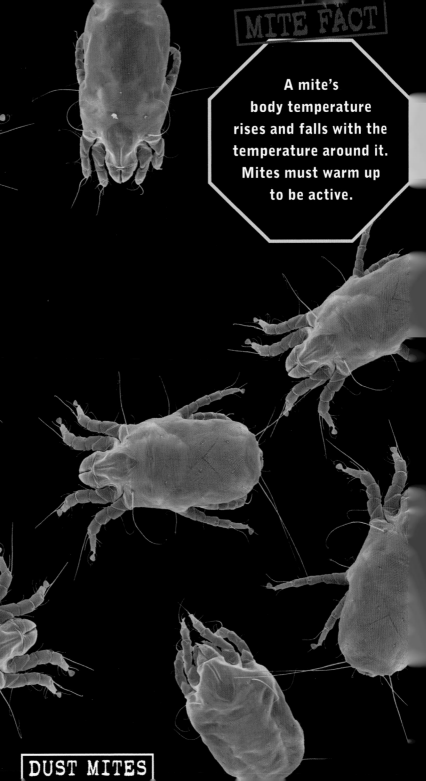

A mite's body temperature rises and falls with the temperature around it. Mites must warm up to be active.

DUST MITES

N THE OUTSIDE

here are about fifty thousand different kinds of mites worldwide. They all share certain features. One is having eir two main body parts fused together. The front part of mite's body is called the prosoma (proh-SOH-mah). At the ont of this is the capitulum (cah-PIH-cheh-luhm). It looks ke a tiny head, but it is really mouthparts. The ite's legs are attached to the prosoma. he back part of the mite's body is lled the opisthosoma (uh-pis-uh-SOH-mah). Take a close ok at the outside of a female vo-spotted spider mite to scover other key features.

LEGS:
These are used for walking, climbing, and holding on. Each leg is covered with short spines and ends in a sharp-tipped claw.

OPISTHOSOMA

EYES:
These organs detect light and send signals to the brain for sight. A mite's eyes are located between the first and second legs. They can probably only tell light from dark. Not all mites have eyes.

PALPS:
The palps stick out on either side of the mouthparts. Palps are covered with sensors that help the mite find food. Palps cover and protect the hypostome and fold back when the mite is feeding.

CHELICERAE (keh-LIH-seh-ree): These are a pair of small clawlike parts near the mouth.

HYPOSTOME (HIGH-poh-stohm): This needlelike part below the chelicerae stabs into the opening made by the chelicerae.

CAPITULUM

PROSOMA

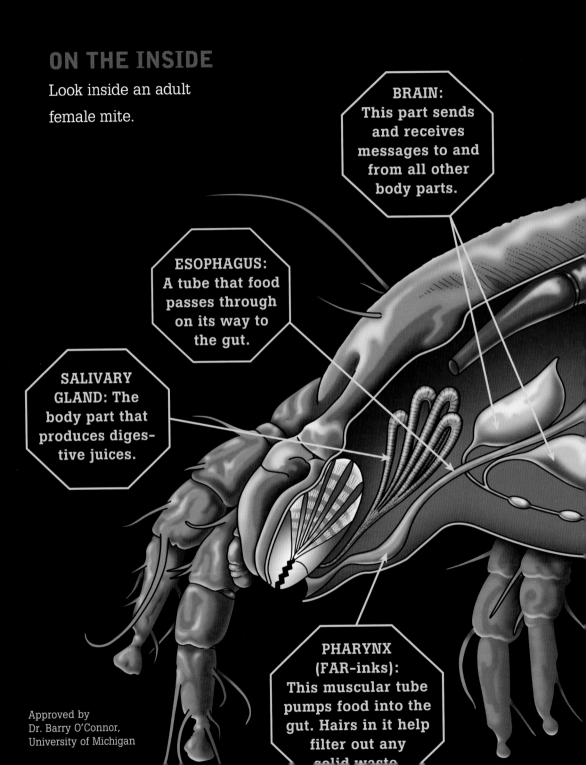

ON THE INSIDE

Look inside an adult
female mite.

BRAIN:
This part sends
and receives
messages to and
from all other
body parts.

ESOPHAGUS:
A tube that food
passes through
on its way to
the gut.

**SALIVARY
GLAND:** The
body part that
produces diges-
tive juices.

**PHARYNX
(FAR-inks):**
This muscular tube
pumps food into the
gut. Hairs in it help
filter out any
solid waste.

Approved by
Dr. Barry O'Connor,
University of Michigan

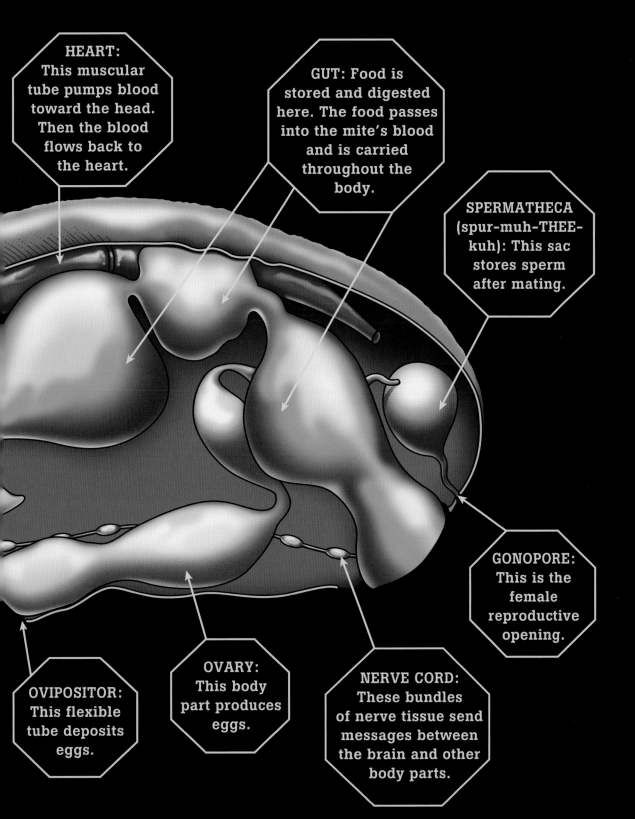

HEART: This muscular tube pumps blood toward the head. Then the blood flows back to the heart.

GUT: Food is stored and digested here. The food passes into the mite's blood and is carried throughout the body.

SPERMATHECA (spur-muh-THEE-kuh): This sac stores sperm after mating.

GONOPORE: This is the female reproductive opening.

OVIPOSITOR: This flexible tube deposits eggs.

OVARY: This body part produces eggs.

NERVE CORD: These bundles of nerve tissue send messages between the brain and other body parts.

BECOMING ADULTS

Like all arachnids, baby mites become adults through incomplete metamorphosis. *Metamorphosis* means "change." A mite's life includes four stages: egg, larva, nymph, and adult.

Except for having six legs instead of eight, mite larvae look and behave much like small adults. The main difference is that, unlike adults, larvae and nymphs are not able to reproduce.

Most kinds of mites go through three different nymph stages. During each stage, the nymph eats and grows until its exoskeleton becomes tight. Then the nymph molts, meaning its exoskeleton splits open and the nymph crawls out. It already has a new exoskeleton covering its body. This new exoskeleton is soft at first. The nymph's heart pumps blood to expand its body before the exoskeleton hardens. Then the nymph has room to grow before it has to molt again. Once its reproductive organs develop, the nymph molts for a final time and becomes an adult. Mites grow up fast. They become adults in a few days or a few weeks after hatching.

SOME ARTHROPODS GO THROUGH COMPLETE METAMORPHOSIS. The four stages are egg, larva, pupa, and adult. Each stage looks and behaves very differently.

MITE FACT

In some kinds of mites, like *Spinturnix americanus*, the females hold their eggs and larvae inside their bodies. The nymphs are born alive.

PLANT EATERS

Many kinds of mites, like these red mites, feed on plant juices. Plants make food in their leaves and store it in the stem and root. The mites' mouthparts are designed to snip open a spot on a plant, like the surface of a leaf. This creates a hollow 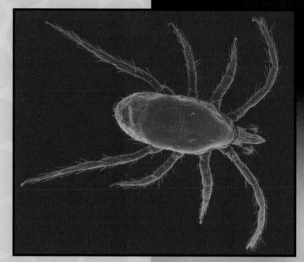 in the leaf and breaks open tubes carrying food made by the leaf. The plant's juices pool in the little hollow the bite creates. The mite sucks in this food.

When a whole colony of mites is feeding, the part of the plant they are eating dies. If the colony grows large enough, the whole plant dies. Red mites are worldwide pests. They feed on as many as three hundred different kinds of plants. In the United States, red mites are a serious threat to cotton plants, citrus trees, vegetables, and a lot of greenhouse plants, like roses.

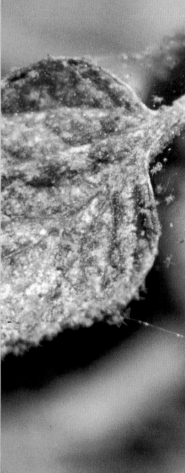

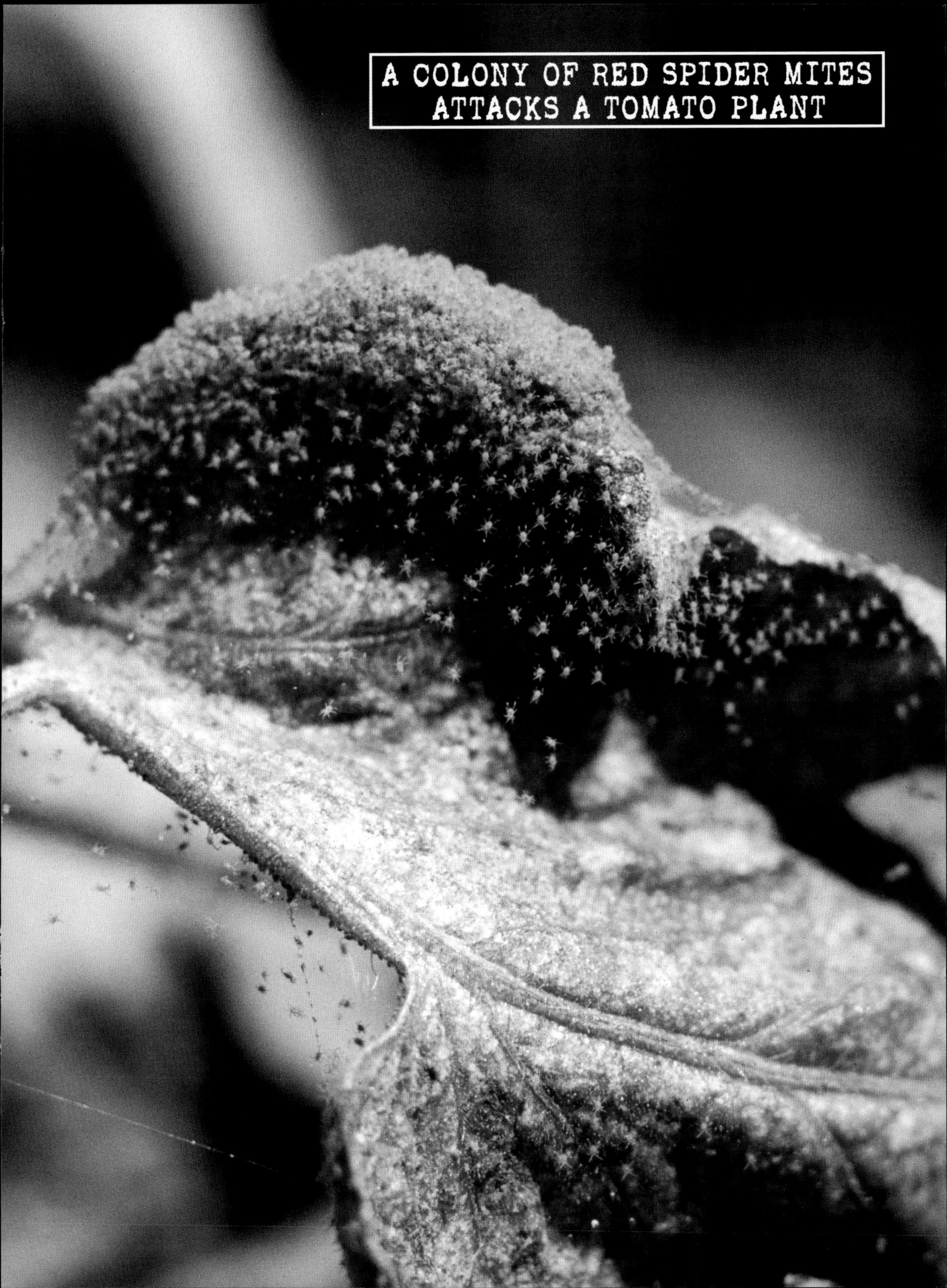
A COLONY OF RED SPIDER MITES ATTACKS A TOMATO PLANT

Gall mites, like these, are so tiny they aren't easy to see unless they're magnified. The mites feed off leaf tissue. They only have two pairs of legs, but these are just right for gripping and holding onto a leaf's surface.

Where winters are cold and trees lose their leaves, the adults stay safe all winter inside cracks in the tree's bark. As the weather warms up and tree buds open, the mites crawl onto a leaf's lower surface and begin to feed.

MITE FACT

Wind spreads gall mites from leaf to leaf and to other trees.

AN EXTREME CLOSE-UP OF A GALL MITE

At each spot where a gall mite is feeding, leaf tissue grows out from the leaf's upper surface. This forms a pouchlike bump, called a gall, around the mite *(below)*. This keeps the mite safely out of sight of predators, like hunting mites. But the gall has an opening on the lower leaf surface. This opening lets males enter to mate with females. Then the female gall mites each deposit hundreds of eggs and die. Gall mite nymphs hatch in about a week. The nymphs continue feeding inside the gall. Finally, they chew their way out of the gall, go to new leaves, and start the cycle over.

PREDATORS

Some mites, like these red velvet mites, are predators. They hunt and eat prey (other living things), usually insects or other mites. Red velvet mites live in dry areas of Africa, Asia, Europe, and North America. Female red velvet mites are some of the largest kinds of mites, about 0.39 inches (1 centimeter) long—as big as an average raisin. Although the mite has a hard exoskeleton, it gets some of the oxygen it needs through lots of tiny slits. These slits mean the exoskeleton leaks moisture, so the mite's body may dry out. Adult red velvet mites live in underground burrows until it rains. Then they come out to hunt and feed. This red velvet mite grabbed and killed its prey with its clawlike chelicerae.

Whirligig mites got their nickname because of the way they move in a spiral path while searching for prey. These mites lay their eggs under bits of tree bark and in leaf litter. Once the eggs hatch, the nymphs of the whirligig mites crawl up plants and onto leaves. There they hunt anything small enough for them to catch. They eat by poking their mouthparts through the prey's exoskeleton and sucking out the prey's body juices. The whirligig hunts lots of plant-eating mites and insects, such as this aphid. So farmers and gardeners value whirligig mites.

WHIRLIGIG MITE

PARASITES

Still other kinds of mites are parasites. They get the food they need by living on other living things. Below are hair follicle mites. A hair follicle is a small tube containing the hair's root. The human host doesn't even know the mites are there. And when people keep clean, the mites don't increase in number enough to cause itching. A hair follicle mite has a wormlike body with four pairs of legs near its mouth. It crawls into a hair follicle and feeds on the body oils that collect there. A number of hair follicle mites may feed together. They're easily passed on when people touch or share clothes or towels.

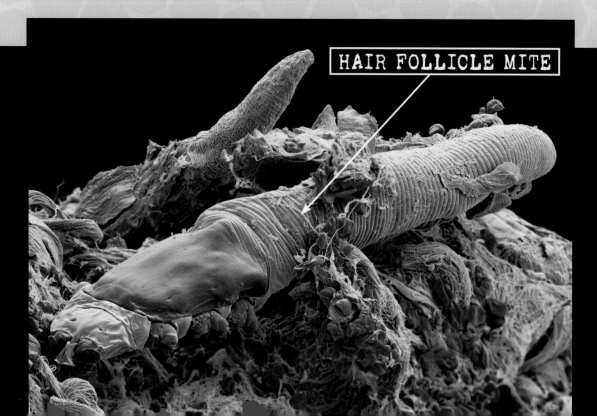

HAIR FOLLICLE MITE

Dust mites mainly eat human skin. But they eat the bits that naturally flake off every day. These bits and the mites that eat them are too tiny to see with the naked eye. Dust mites can cause an allergic reaction in some people. When this happens, people sneeze, cough, and have a runny nose. The dust mites themselves don't cause problems. Their wastes do.

Dust mites have very short digestive systems. Their food is only partly digested by the time it passes out of their bodies. The partly digested waste pellets are nearly as big as the mites themselves. The dust mites continue their digestion process by eating the pellets up to four times. Sometimes the pellets are carried away by air currents.

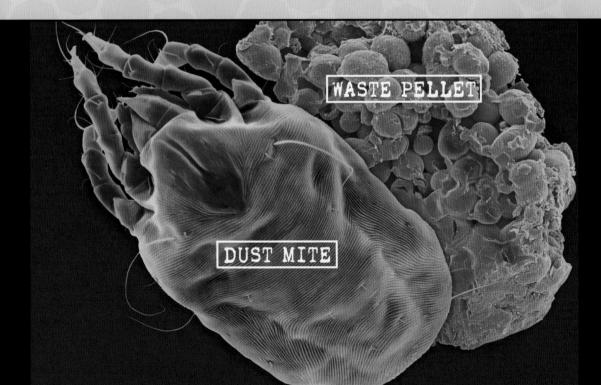

As nymphs and adults, chigger mites hunt insects and other arachnids or eat their eggs. However, a chigger's six-legged larval stage feeds on the skin of an animal or a human host. A chigger larva must find a host or die.

Chigger adults lay their eggs in leaf litter. Once the chigger larva hatches, it climbs a blade of grass or a lump of soil and waits. When it senses people or animals close by, it lifts its front legs. If an animal or a person brushes against it, the chigger larva grabs on *(below)*.

The chigger larva's mouthparts snip into the host's skin. Then the larva brings up a little of its own spit. This spit has chemicals that make the host's skin into liquid. Then the chigger larva sucks in this liquid meal. The larva's spit causes the skin around the feeding site to form a sort of tube. The longer the chigger larva feeds, the deeper the larva goes into the host's skin. If nothing happens to knock the chigger larva off, it will feed for several days. By then the bite site is red, and the skin has a very itchy bump. The larva's saliva causes an allergic reaction that makes the host's skin itch. When the chigger larva drops off its host, it molts and becomes a nymph.

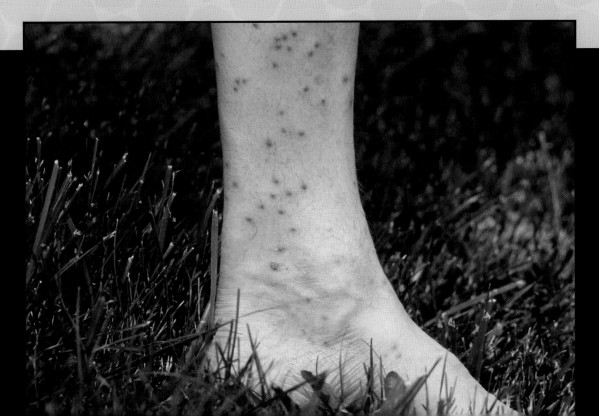

Adult varroa (VUH-ruh-wuh) mites are about the size of a pinhead. They are parasites on honeybees. These mites use their mouthparts to pierce the bee's exoskeleton and feed on the bee's blood.

After mating, an adult female varroa mite entered a wax cell in a honeybee hive. The bee egg in this cell hatched into a larva. The bee larva has become ready for the pupal stage. This is the stage where it changes into an adult honeybee. Worker bees cover the cell with a wax cap. The bee pupa and the mite are in it. Inside the cell, the female varroa mite lays from four to six eggs on the honeybee pupa. These soon hatch. The mite nymphs

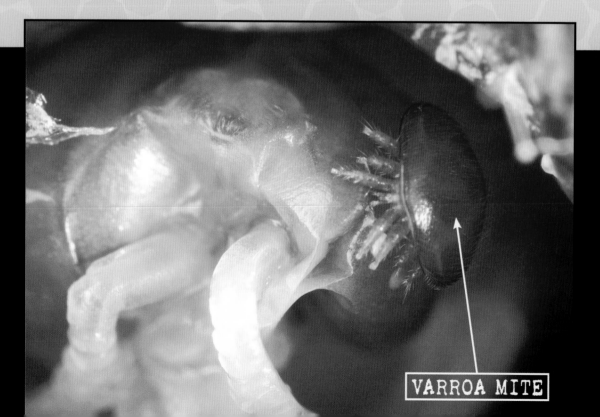

VARROA MITE

and their mother feed by piercing the pupa's exoskeleton and
sucking its blood. This usually doesn't kill the pupa.

Several of the nymphs will become adult
mites and mate just before the adult
bee emerges from the cell. The adult
mites continue to feed on the adult
bee's blood. The old female mite
and the males soon die. The
young female varroa mites drop
off the bee, find a new bee larva,
and continue the mite's life cycle.

MITE FACT

In the past
thirty years, varroa
mites have harmed honeybee
colonies throughout the world.
One treatment that helps kill
varroa mites is an oil made
from thyme, an herb used
to season food.

VARROA MITE

Not all parasitic mites live on the outside of their host. This sarcoptic (sar-KOP-tik) mange mite is living inside its host's skin. After mating, the female mite burrows deep into the skin of her host. She makes a tunnel as much as 1 inch (2.5 cm) long. She feeds by snipping into the skin and sucking the clear body fluid that floods in. She soon lays as many as fifty eggs. Then she dies. The larvae hatch, leave the burrow, and dig tunnels of their own. There they feed and grow up to mate and continue the life cycle.

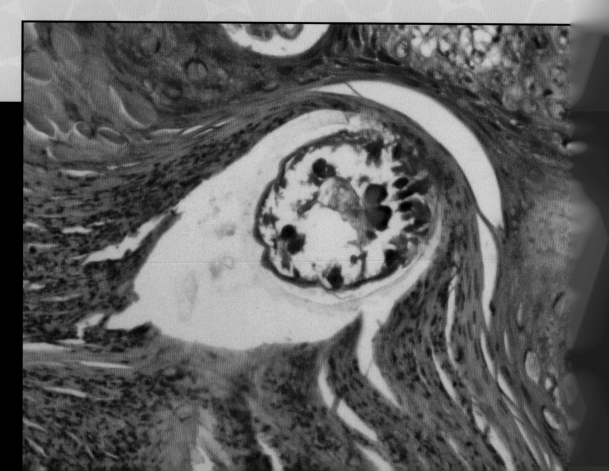

The spit a sarcoptic mange mite releases as it feeds
makes the host's skin itch. The skin becomes scaly. Then
the host animal's hair falls out, causing bald patches *(below)*.
Mange mites can be killed with chemicals prescribed by
a veterinarian. The vet usually drips the medicine on the
infected spot. Or the vet might give the infected animal a
bath with the medicines in it. This dog has mange, but, after
treatment, it will be healthy again.

One kind of sarcoptic mite attacks humans. The problem this causes is called scabies (SKAY-beez). These mites are called scabies mites. After mating, the adult female scabies mites *(below)* burrow into a person's skin. They create a tunnel just below the skin's surface by feeding on the skin tissue. As they tunnel, the females deposit their eggs behind them. The larvae hatch in about a week, move up to the surface of the skin, and into hair follicles. There, they molt and become nymphs. The nymphs feed and molt in the hair follicles. They become adults in about a week. The adult scabies mites may live about a month. They feed by making short tunnels into the host's skin. Then they mate and the life cycle begins again.

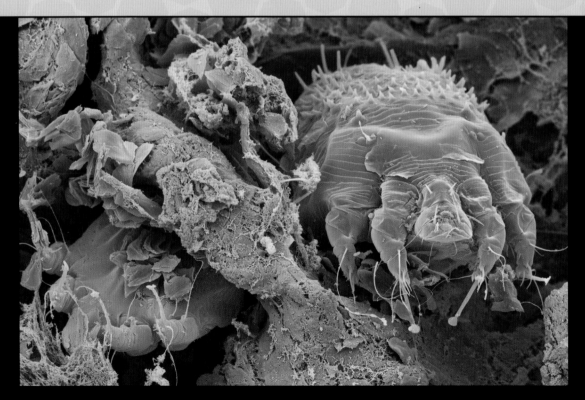

Scabies mites spread easily from person to person. They spread when people touch or share clothes, towels, or beds. Small bumps appear where the female mites enter the skin. These spots and the tunnels cause extreme itching. In severe cases, large areas of the skin may become scaly and flaky *(below)*. A special chemical lotion can kill scabies mites. The person with the scabies covers the affected skin with the lotion. The next day, the person showers off the lotion. The lotion needs to be put on again a week later—about the time any eggs would hatch. To prevent the spread of this mite, furniture and flooring need to be cleaned with disinfectants. Bedding and clothes must be washed in hot water.

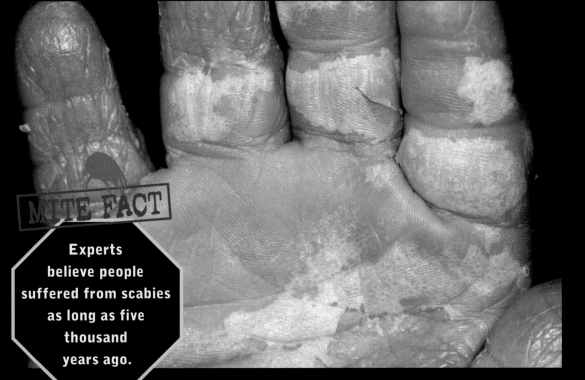

MITE FACT

Experts believe people suffered from scabies as long as five thousand years ago.

ONE MITE GENERATION

It's a warm August afternoon in Illinois. The female two-spotted spider mite is feeding on the lower surface of a bean plant leaf. Her sharp-tipped feet let her hold on tight. Her mouthparts are needle sharp too. She uses them to pierce one of the leaf's cells, the tiny building blocks of the leaf. She feeds by sucking out the plant's juices. Then she moves on and feeds on another plant cell.

MITE FACT

The two-spotted spider mite's body is clear. The two spots are really balls of waste inside its body. The wastes are shed with each molt.

The two-spotted spider mite is tiny—only about 0.02 inches (0.5 millimeters) long. If she was feeding alone, the little mite wouldn't harm the plant. However, she's one of many. The leaf is so crowded with mites, most of the plant cells are already empty. So the female two-spotted spider mite moves on to a fresh leaf to feed.

As she travels, the mite produces liquid silk from its pedipalps near its mouth. As she touches this silk to something and pulls, the liquid silk becomes a strong line. She deposits silk while she walks along. She holds onto this silk with her feet to keep from falling. At the edge of the leaf, she shoots out more silk. A gentle breeze catches the silk strand and carries her along. This is the way she rides across the space separating two leaves. The silk trail she lays down becomes a bridge for other two-spotted mites to cross. She continues on, walking on silk webbing laid down by other two-spotted spider mites.

When the female next stops to feed, a male two-spotted spider mite comes close. Male two-spotted spider mites only mate with female two-spotted spider mates. This female helped her mate find her. She coated some of her silk with pheromones. These are special chemicals that attract males. As he walks up to her, she stays still and allows him to climb on her back. He inserts a tubelike part into her body. He passes sperm (male reproductive cells) through the tube. When a sperm merges with one of her egg cells, a baby two-spotted spider mite begins to develop.

MITE FACT

Males are even smaller than females. They are also narrower, and their tail ends are more pointed.

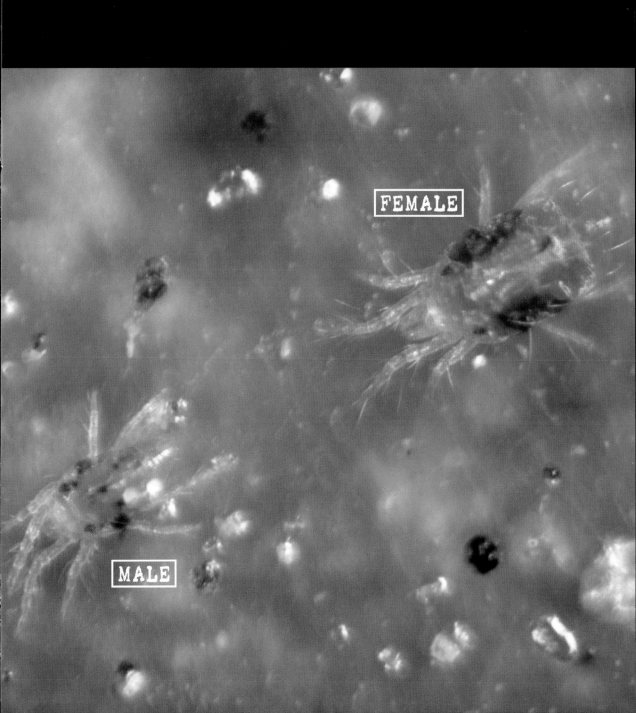

After mating, the female begins to deposit her eggs. She deposits from five to ten eggs a day, laying a total of about one hundred eggs. Although she only lives about a month, the adult female lays several hundred eggs before dying. The eggs are slightly sticky. She tacks them to the silk webbing crisscrossing the leaf she's on. Eggs develop fastest when the air is warm and wet—about 80°F (26°C) with around 50 percent humidity. Just two days after the eggs are laid, six-legged larvae hatch. Of course, not all the eggs survive to hatch. Insects and predatory mites *(facing page)* eat lots of mite eggs.

MITE FACT

The mite's silk webbing helps hide eggs, young, and adults from predators. It also shields them from chemicals sprayed on plants to kill mites.

POPULATION EXPLOSION

Over the following week, the six-legged two-spotted spider mite larvae grow and molt to become eight-legged nymphs. Eating and growing bigger, the nymphs molt three times over the next week. The males mature faster than the females. So they're ready to mate as soon as the females are ready to lay eggs. In less than a month, another life cycle is completed. With such a short life cycle, two-spotted spider mites may go through as many as twenty generations in a summer. As the population increases, the mites spread out. They feed on the upper surface as well as the lower surface of leaves of this bean plant *(right)*. With larvae, nymphs, and adults all sucking juices from the plant's cells, the two-spotted spider mites can seriously weaken the plant.

In September the days get cooler and shorter. The bean plant nears the end of its growing period. At that time, the generation of adult two-spotted spider mites that develops is very different. For one thing, they are orange. The orange-colored mites *(inset)* store fat as they feed.

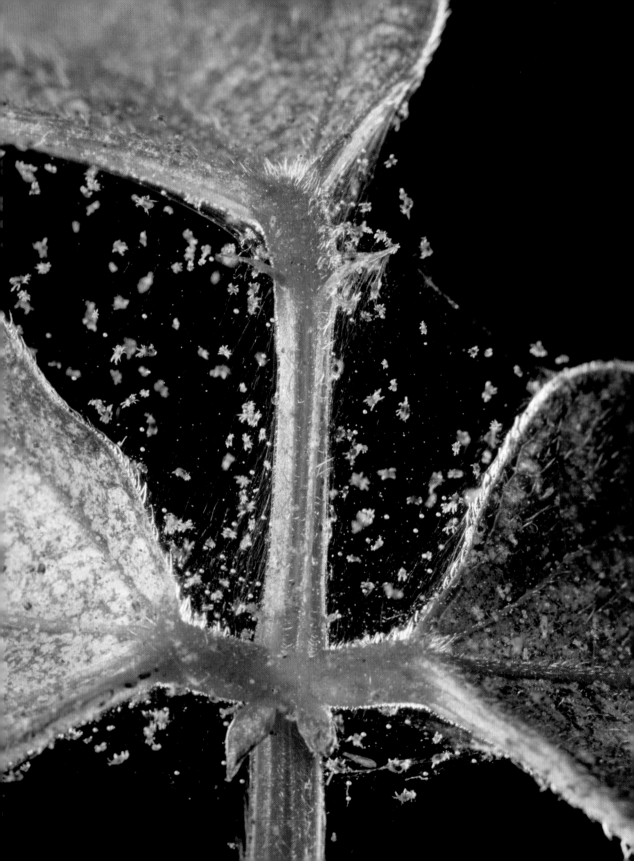

WINTERING OVER

As the days continue to shorten, the orange adults mate and crawl down the plant's stem. On the ground, they find sheltered places among the bits of leaf litter or crawl into cracks in the earth. There, each adult hibernates. This means its body slows down so much it doesn't need to feed.

When the days lengthen and warm up in the spring, the adults become active again. Because they're smaller and store less fat, few males survive. But the females had already mated in the fall. They're ready to lay eggs. A newly emerged female quickly finds a plant home, crawls up the stem, and starts to feed on a leaf. Over the next week, she deposits about one hundred eggs. In just a few days, larvae, like this one, are hatching. And before the female dies, the mite's cycle of life has begun again.

MITE FACT

Two-spotted spider mites feed on as many as two hundred different kinds of plants.

AN EXTREME CLOSEUP OF A SPIDER MITE

MITES AND OTHER SNEAKY LITTLE ARACHNIDS

MITES BELONG TO A GROUP, or order, of arachnids called Acari (AHK-air-ee). There are about fifty thousand different kinds currently known worldwide. However, scientists believe there may actually be as many as a million different kinds. Most mites are tiny. Some can only be seen with a microscope. The largest are the size of an average raisin. Ticks are a type of mite and are among the biggest kinds.

SCIENTISTS GROUP living and extinct animals with others that are similar. So mites are classified this way:

> kingdom: Animalia
> phylum: Arthropoda
> class: Arachnida
> order: Acari

HELPFUL OR HARMFUL? Mites are both, but they're mainly harmful because they live at the expense of other living things. Their small size lets mites go unnoticed by their host. If they live on plants, predators aren't likely to find them. Some kinds of mites are helpful because there are lots of them and they become prey for other predators, such as wasps.

HOW BIG IS a two–spotted mite? A female is about 0.02 inches (0.5 mm) long.

MORE SNEAKY LITTLE ARACHNIDS

Mites use their size to be sneaky. But they aren't the only little arachnids. Compare the advantage mites get from being small to how being little helps these arachnids.

Little thief spiders of New Zealand are only 0.06 inches (2 mm) long.

This spider takes advantage of being tiny to steal much bigger prey than it could safely catch for itself. The spider locates a large orb weaver spider's web and lurks, waiting for a flying insect to be caught. It continues to wait while the big spider runs across its web and stabs the prey with its fangs. This injects venom (liquid poison) and paralyzes the prey. If the orb weaver leaves this prey to attack other prey, the little thief runs onto the big spider's web. The little thief spins threads of its own to the prey and bites to snip the prey out of the orb weaver's web. Then the little thief dines on its stolen food. Check out this website to see the little thief spider in action: http://www.maniacworld.com/thief-spider-at-work. html.

Bone Cave harvestmen are found only in caves and sinkholes in

Texas. They are very sensitive to drying out. So they are found only in the coolest, dampest spots in these underground places. Less than 0.125 inches (2.7 mm) long and blind, this tiny harvestman is still good at finding even tinier insects. Being so small, the Bone Cave harvestman is able to survive on a food source too small for most bigger animals to waste energy catching. Imagine how small this harvestman's babies are and what tiny insects they must prey on!

# GLOSSARY

adult: the final stage of an arachnid's life cycle. An arachnid is able to reproduce at this stage.

brain: the organ that receives messages from body parts and sends signals to control them

capitulum: the headlike part of a mite that has the mouthparts and the palps

chelicerae: a pair of strong, jawlike parts that extend from the head in front of the mouth

colony: a group of animals of the same kind that live together

disinfectants: liquids that get rid of harmful germs

egg: a female reproductive cell; also the name given to the first stage of an arachnid's life cycle

esophagus: a tube through which food passes on its way to the stomach

exoskeleton: the protective, armorlike covering on the outside of the body

eyes: the sensory organs that detect light and send signals to the brain for sight. Some mites lack eyes. Those with eyes may have from one to five.

gonopore: the female reproductive opening

gut: the tubes where food is stored and digested before passing into the mite's blood. Mites have three different guts.

hair follicle: a small tube containing a hair's root

heart: the muscular tube that pumps blood throughout the body

hibernation: the state in which an animal's body slows down so much that it doesn't need to feed

host: an animal or plant on or in which another thing lives

hypostome: a needlelike part below the chelicerae

larva: the first immature, six-legged stage of a mite's life

legs: limbs used for walking, climbing, and hanging onto a host. Most mites have eight although some, like gall mites, have only two pairs.

molt: the process of an arachnid shedding its exoskeleton

mouthparts: these may be shaped for biting, stinging, sucking, or sawing, depending on the feeding behavior of different kinds of mites

nerve cord: bundles of nerve tissue that send messages between the brain and other body parts

nymph: the second immature stage of the mite's life cycle. The nymph has eight legs and looks and behaves much like an adult. However, it is smaller and unable to reproduce.

opisthosoma: the back part of a mite's body

ovary: the body part that produces eggs

ovipositor: a flexible tube that can be extended outside the body to deposit eggs

palps: the parts on either side of the mouthparts of some mites

parasite: a living thing that gets what it needs to survive at the expense of other living things

pharynx: a muscular body part that contracts to create a pumping force, drawing food into the body's digestive system

pheromones: chemical smells given off as a form of communication

predator: an animal that catches and kills other animals to eat

prey: an animal eaten by a predator

prosoma: the front part of a mite's body. It is separated from the back part, the opisthosoma, by only a narrow groove. The prosoma includes the capitulum and the legs.

salivary gland: an organ that produces digestive juices

sperm: a male reproductive cell

spermatheca: the sac in female arachnids that stores sperm after mating

DIGGING DEEPER

To keep on investigating mites, explore these books and online sites.

BOOKS

Gleason, Carrie. *Feasting Bedbugs, Mites, and Ticks*. Saint Catharines, ON: Crabtree Publishing, 2010. Investigate the tiny insects and arachnids that live on humans.

Jarrow, Gail. *Chiggers*. Farmington Hills, MI: KidHaven, 2003. Learn more about a little mite that causes a big itch while feasting on its host's skin cells.

Lew, Kristi. *Itch & Ooze: Gross Stuff on Your Skin*. Minneapolis: Millbrook Press, 2010. Learn more about mites, chiggers, and other critters that can live on or in your skin.

Stewart, Melissa. *Do People Really Have Tiny Insects Living in Their Eyelashes?: And Other Question about the Microscopic World*. Minneapolis: Lerner Publications Company, 2011. Explore the microscopic world in this fun question-and-answer book.

MORE FROM SANDRA MARKLE

ARACHNID WORLD:
Black Widows
Harvestmen
Orb Weavers
Scorpions
Ticks
Wolf Spiders

WEBSITES

Mites

http://www.sel.barc.usda.gov/acari/frames/mites.html

Take a close-up look at mites that affect people, animals, and crops at the United States Department of Agriculture website.

Mites That Bother People

http://www.the-piedpiper.co.uk/th5i.htm#bedmite

Investigate mites that make people itch and feel sick. Find out treatments for these pests and how to avoid being attacked.

Mites Videos with KidPort Reference Library

http://www.kidport.com/RefLib/Science/Videos/Animals/Arachnids/Mite.htm

Learn more about mites, and check out the videos to see some in action.

WLOS Bee Mite Story

http://wn.com/WLOS_Bee_Mite_story

Watch bees being checked for mites. Find out how beehives are being treated to protect the bees from bee-killing mites.

LERNER 𝒆 SOURCE™

Visit www.lernerresource.com for free, downloadable arachnid diagrams, research assignments to use with this series, and additional information about arachnid scientific names.

MITE ACTIVITY

Although each two-spotted spider mite is small, it can cause a lot of damage to plants. Follow these steps to get a feel for why this mite can be such a big problem.

1. Cut as big a leaf shape as you can from a single sheet of green paper.

2. Use a hole punch to make five white circles from a sheet of white typing paper. These represent five female two-spotted spider mites. Scatter them as far apart as possible on the big green leaf.

3. Next, punch out five circles—eggs—for each female. Place these close to each female.

4. Repeat, punching out five more pretend eggs per female and place them on your leaf close to their pretend mothers.

You need to repeat this process at least two more times to get an idea how a two-spotted spider mite population multiplies. Even if only half of this population is female and survives to reproduce, the population quickly explodes. And each larva, nymph, and adult is sucking plant juices out of the leaf. This reduces the amount of food the plant gets for itself.

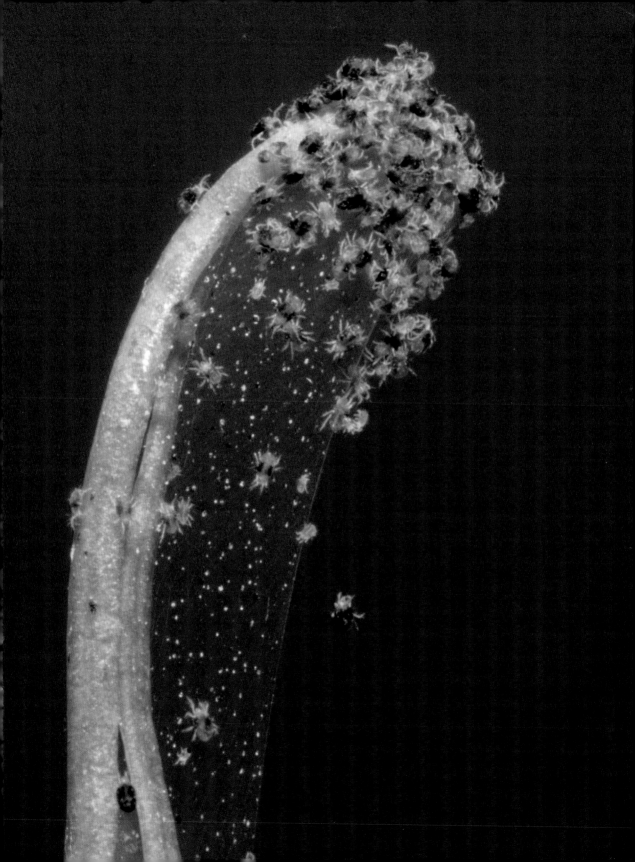

INDEX

PHOTO ACKNOWLEDGMENTS

The images in this book are used with the permission of: © Albert Lleal/Minden Pictures, p. 4; © Dr. Dennis Kunkel Microscopy, Inc./Visuals Unlimited, Inc., pp. 5, 12, 14, 19, 20; © LADA/ARS/USDA/Photo Researchers, Inc., pp. 6–7; © Laura Westlund/Independent Picture Service, pp. 8–9; © Nigel Cattlin/Visuals Unlimited, Inc., pp. 11, 28, 30–31, 33, 36, 36–37; © Alan Weaving/ardea.com, pp. 12–13; © Donald Specker/Animals Animals, p. 15; © Beverly Joubert/National Geographic/Getty Images, p. 16; © Harold Taylor/ Oxford Scientific/Getty Images, p. 17; © Eye of Science/Photo Researchers, Inc., pp. 18, 25; © David M. Dennis/Animals Animals, p. 21; © Crown Copyright courtesy of Central Science Laboratory/Photo Researchers, Inc., p. 22; © Science Source/Photo Researchers, Inc., p. 23; © Daniel Snyder/Visuals Unlimited, Inc., p. 24; © Deddeda Deddeda/Photolibrary, p. 25; © Dr. Ken Greer/Visuals Unlimited, Inc., p. 27; © Nigel Cattlin/Alamy, pp. 29, 35; © Dr. Martin Oeggerli/Visuals Unlimited, Inc., p. 38; © Simon Pollard, p. 41 (top); © William R. Elliott, p. 41 (bottom); © Animals Animals/SuperStock, p. 47.

Front cover: © Eye of Science/Photo Researchers, Inc.

Main body text set in Glypha LT Std 55 Roman 12/20. Typeface provided by Adobe Systems.